POVILAITIS

Just Us GIRLS

Just Us GIRLS

secrets to feeling good about yourself, inside and out

Moka
with Melissa Daly
illustrated by Éric Héliot

sunscreen

Book series designed by Higashi Glaser Design

Library of Congress Cataloging-in-Publication data has been applied for.

ISBN: 0-8109-9161-6

Text copyright © 2004 Moka with Melissa Daly
Illustrations copyright © 2003 Éric Heliot

Translated by Jack Hawkes

Published in 2004 by Amulet Books
an imprint of Harry N. Abrams, Incorporated
100 Fifth Avenue
New York, NY 10011
www.abramsbooks.com

Printed and bound in China
10 9 8 7 6 5 4 3 2 1

Abrams is a subsidiary of
LA MARTINIÈRE

Special thanks Dr. Martine Cohen, gynecologist,
and Mrs. Fabienne Roy, physical therapist, for their help.

contents

phase 2:

ME FIRST!

phase 3:

ME AND EVERYONE ELSE

WILL I EVER BE NORMAL? WILL I EVER BE HAPPY?

Don't you wish someone could just give you all the answers? The problem is you don't even know who to ask. That's where this book comes in. It can't predict the future, but it'll help you get to know your body—and yourself—a little bit better, so you can learn how to be the best you possible!

After all, there are a lot of things about growing up that you just don't want to talk about with other people—sometimes not even your friends. They're just things you have to face on your own. You'll find some guidance in these pages, practical information, medical advice . . . and a little humor, because not everything has to be a great tragedy!

So go through it from cover to cover, or pick and choose what applies to you. Keep it on the shelf and come back to it when a new slew of questions pops up in your head. It'll be there, ready to lend a helping hand whenever you need it.

ph1

THE STRANGE

you and your hair:
a love/hate relationship

hormones, you're
making me crazy

CLOTHES MAKE
THE WOMAN

WORLD

your body's playing tricks on you . . .

OF THE BODY

**BIG, SMALL,
SHORT, TALL . . .
you're never
happy**

your period

for the time being, you're still a girl. But in just a few years, you'll hardly recognize yourself. That's because your body is going through a huge transformation process called puberty. This is the time when your body becomes capable of reproduction, or of having a baby. To get puberty started, the genital organs and a gland in your brain called the pituitary secrete hormones that circulate throughout the body in the blood, triggering various changes. Getting through puberty can be a little confusing, but it won't take too long before you're used to the new you.

Getting your first period—or beginning menstruation—is one of the most important events of puberty. Your period will probably appear when you're between eleven and fourteen years old, although it might happen a little earlier or a little later than that. When you get it may depend on your weight: girls who are very thin tend to get their periods later than those who are heavier. But don't freak out if your best friend gets hers before you get yours—every girl is different. There might not be any warning signals before your period arrives. Or you might notice a little cramping in your lower abdomen, as if you ate too much Mexican food last night. You might also feel some soreness in your breasts, even if you don't really have any yet. (Growth of breasts and the beginning of menstruation usually happen around the same time.)

ph1

12

Do I measure up to everyone else??

Some girls have lower-back pain before they get their period; others' legs feel kind of heavy. The symptoms sound like a pain (literally!), but for most women they're really not that bad. In fact, many women don't feel any different at all during their period.

However, there are some women who have more severe symptoms, such as painful cramps. If you turn out to be one of them, there are plenty of effective remedies—such as taking pain-reliever pills with ibuprofen (but avoiding aspirin, since it thins the blood too much), drinking certain herbal teas, and cutting back on caffeinated drinks. Putting a heating pad on your stomach works great, too. And don't be embarrassed to ask your mom for advice. She's been having her period for years, so she'll know just what to do!

A normal menstrual cycle lasts twenty-eight days (that means you'll start your period once every twenty-eight days or so). Menstruation itself lasts between three and six days. But your first few periods may be irregular—that is, they may come once every two months, or last for two days during one cycle and eight days the next. This is totally normal: your body is like a rookie player, still getting used to the new stuff it's supposed to do.

When you start menstruating, you'll have to use maxi-pads (official name: sanitary napkins) or tampons during the day and at night. If you use maxi-pads, you'll stick the pad inside your underwear, and it will catch and absorb the menstrual blood as it comes out. You should change it at least every four to eight hours, or whenever it seems to be too full to absorb any more.

If you prefer, you can use tampons instead, although it takes most girls a little practice before they get the hang of inserting one. (You'll know if it's not in the right place because it will feel pretty uncomfortable.) Because of that, most girls wait a year or two before trying them, but you can start right from your first period if you want to. Most women find tampons more comfortable and convenient, since they're inserted into the vagina and absorb the blood before it comes out of the body. While you can swim and play sports while using a pad, it's a lot nicer-feeling with a tampon. Just as with pads, you should remove the used tampon and put in a new one every four to eight hours, or sooner if it's full and can't absorb any more (you'll know because blood will start to

leak onto your underwear). You don't have to take the tampon out to pee, but you should remove it after eight hours or you'll be at risk for a rare bacteria-related disease called toxic shock syndrome. And in case you were wondering, using tampons doesn't mean you're not a virgin anymore—you have to have sexual intercourse to lose your virginity.

Before your period, you'll probably notice a whitish, mucus-like discharge in your underwear. This is also totally normal; you don't need to do anything about it. But if you ever have really bad itching or burning, you should see your doctor. It may nothing, but it could be an infection, which can be easily treated by a doctor.

...and what

Look out, Madonna! Here I come!

ADONNA

HELIOT

comes with it

Lots of other things happen around the time you start menstruating. For one thing, your breasts begin to grow. And that means . . . time to shop for your first bra! The ones that will feel most comfortable at first are those made of cotton. Good first-time bras are often labeled "training bras." Some stores offer bra fittings. A salesperson will measure your chest and select bras for you to try on. If this sounds too embarrassing, you can also have your mom or an older sister help you pick the right bra. It shouldn't feel like it's cutting into your skin or so loose that it will shift around when you move. But even the best-fitting bra will take some getting used to. Believe it or not, though, one day you'll wear one without even thinking about it.

Another change you'll notice is that you start to perspire, or sweat, more. Perspiration has no odor when it first comes out of your body, but

Suddenly I remember Grandma's leek soup...

it breaks down when it comes into contact with air and starts to smell not so great. Because of this, you'll probably want to start showering more often, especially after exercising or playing sports, and eventually use an antiperspirant/deodorant. In really rare cases, a person will sweat a lot—way more than normal. If you think you've got this problem, ask your doctor about it on your next visit. There are certain special prescription antiperspirants he or she can give you to deal with this.

If you're not already, you should get into the habit of changing your underwear every day. Sweat "down there" can be especially fragrant! Chances are no one will notice but you, but you'll just feel better when you're clean and fresh.

The skeletal system also grows—you'll probably reach your full height during puberty. Muscles become firmer and more prominent. Your hips grow larger. And your thighs and your butt will get rounder, thanks to a new layer of fat. This doesn't mean you are fat—everyone gets this

Your hips grow larger.

Your butt gets rounder.

extra layer, and it's actually necessary in order to menstruate and have babies. If a girl loses too much weight and her body fat decreases too much, she'll stop getting her period, which is really unhealthy. Of course, gaining too much weight is equally unhealthy. You can avoid both of these things by maintaining a healthy lifestyle. That means being physically active, either by working out or playing sports or doing activities you enjoy, like hiking or dancing, and also eating nutritious foods: lots of fruits, vegetables, whole grains, lean meat, and low-fat milk, and not a lot of cookies, candy, or fast food.

And then there's the hair. As if all of this wasn't enough, you're also going to start growing hair under your arms and in your pubic area. Your leg hair may also seem darker and fuller.

If you don't like having hair in your armpits or on your legs, you can always remove it.

Shaving is the easiest and most common way to get rid of hair.

Your muscles get stronger.

Hair grows in new places.

ph1

Other options include depilatory creams (they use chemicals to melt away hair, but aren't always as convenient and effective as shaving), and waxing (where liquid wax is spread on the hair and then ripped off like a Band-Aid after it hardens—ouch!). But removing hair isn't really even necessary. It's just a question of personal preference. In any case, be careful not to irritate your skin. Use moisturizer on your legs and a gentle deodorant on your underarms—there are now some brands made especially for soothing your skin after shaving.

hygiene

As you've probably already figured out, the bathroom is going to play a much more significant role in your life from now on. Obviously you've been bathing your whole life. But now it probably seems even more important to look, smell, and feel good. Showering uses less water and is less drying to the skin than taking a bath, but either way of getting clean is okay.

Anyway, you may have to convince the rest of your family that you have a right, from now on, to take more time in the bathroom. If anyone jokes about your sudden modesty, tell them that you deserve a certain amount of privacy now that you're getting older. Setting up a morning schedule with your brothers and sisters can help, so that everyone knows exactly how long everyone else needs to get ready, and they won't come banging on the door before it's their turn.

"Feminine hygiene," as the TV ads call it, is pretty simple. The best soap to use "down there" is something mild, without a lot of added deodorants or scents or colors. You don't need to buy anything specially made for this purpose—regular soap works just fine. You don't want to use soap inside your genitals, however. In fact, it's best just to use water alone on the vulva (the area around your vagina). Also, when you go to the bathroom, get into the habit of wiping from front to back, that is to say from the genitals toward the anus, to help avoid infection.

Cleanliness is the first step toward beauty—after all, puberty doesn't just involve annoying changes, but ones that bring out your natural good looks as well. So here's some advice that will help you to feel good about the way you look.

your skin

PIMPLES, BLACK-HEADS, ACNE!

These are the sworn enemies of teenagers and grown women alike. And they pop up everywhere—your back, your butt, and, worst of all, your face. They're caused by an excess of sebum (a substance secreted by the skin) along with dirt and bacteria that get trapped inside pores. But your fate is not sealed—you can fight back!

First, you have to keep your skin clean. When washing your face, it's best to use a cleanser specifically made for it—regular body soap is too irritating. There are tons of different facial cleansers on drugstore shelves; look for one that's made for your skin type. If your skin is dry and flaky after washing, you have dry skin. If it feels greasy after washing and throughout the day, and you frequently have pimples, you have oily skin. If it's dry in some places and oily in others, you have combination skin.

PÂTÉ

ph1

22

And that's right, if it's not particularly dry or oily, you have normal skin.

Washing with an exfoliating scrub once a week will also help prevent blemishes by sloughing off the dead skin cells that can block your pores. You might also want to try one of the many products specially made to treat acne—these should contain salicylic acid or benzoyl peroxide. If you wear makeup, don't forget to wash it off every night before you go to bed. Otherwise, you're more likely to get pimples. When you do get whiteheads or blackheads, resist the urge to squeeze them out—it'll only make things worse in the long run. You could end up with permanent scars.

If you're really bothered by your acne, ask your regular doctor to refer you to a dermatologist, a doctor who specializes in skin problems. He or she can prescribe special creams and treatments that have been proven to knock out pimples.

A final, super-important way of taking care of your skin is to wear sunscreen—especially when you go to the beach, but every other day, too. Even if you have dark skin or tan easily, exposing your skin to too much sun can result in wrinkles down the road, and may even cause skin cancer. You should use a sunscreen with SPF 15 or higher—this is crucial for girls with very light-colored skin. Lots of moisturizers and makeup on the market today have sunscreen built right in, so look for that on the label. It's never too early to start taking care of your skin. Pamper it now and in thirty years you'll get compliments on how young and beautiful you look!

If you really, really must have a tan, consider using self-tanners. The new ones won't turn you orange!

your teeth

Lots of kids don't like to brush their teeth—they fight their parents over it every night. But you aren't a kid anymore, and the teeth you have now are the last ones you'll get! Sure, a dentist can fill your cavities, but it's a pretty unpleasant experience, and who wants a mouth full of fillings? To avoid this, it's important to brush after every meal. Unfortunately, you can't always brush after lunch, since you're at school. That just makes it even more important to brush well in the morning and especially at night. You can also chew sugarless gum after a meal when you can't brush—it keeps the saliva flowing, and saliva is good for cleaning teeth. Today, there are even brands of chewing gum made

especially to help keep teeth clean and healthy. (Just don't chew too much, because gum chewing causes you to swallow air. If you feel bloated, or have a stomachache or gas, chewing gum could be the culprit.)

Lots of preteens and teens have to get braces or a retainer to straighten their teeth. It may seem like a bad thing when it happens, but after it comes off, you'll have a gorgeous, straight-toothed smile that will last your whole life.

Even if you don't have any problems with your teeth, you need to see a dentist twice a year. He or she will clean your teeth and make sure that there's nothing wrong. Your teeth will be whiter, and your gums healthier.

You can also make your smile brighter with one of the many tooth-whitening products available at any drugstore. However, they're pretty expensive, and your teeth probably don't really need extra whitening anyway. Finally, don't forget that smoking and drinking coffee or cola can yellow your teeth. Avoiding these things, brushing well, and seeing the dentist regularly will guarantee you a beautiful smile.

your hair

It might surprise you, but you shouldn't wash your hair too much! Lots of washing and blow-drying can make it brittle, dry, and easily breakable. In some countries, girls only wash their hair once a week! Still, most of us here like to do it every day. If you do shampoo every day and have trouble with frizz and fly-away hair, consider switching to every other day and just rinsing your hair in warm water on the days off. A little conditioner on the ends will keep it combable. And whenever you can get away with air-drying your hair, it's good to give it a break from the heat of the blow dryer.

There are about as many brands of shampoo and conditioner out there as there are people; it's up to you to choose the one which best

suits you. So experiment—that's part of the fun! As for brushes, the best ones are those made from boar bristles or other natural fibers. Those made with steel or plastic bristles are more likely to damage your hair or cause static electricity.

Whether long or short, curly or straight, a great head of hair can make you feel great about yourself! That's why an incredible new cut can give you such a confidence boost. Choose your new look by going through magazines and cutting out pictures you like. Bring these to the salon with you—you don't want to be taken advantage of by an overly creative stylist. Some hairdressers will listen to you, but others will want to do whatever they like! So be very clear and firm about how you want to look. Don't worry about the hairdresser's feelings—you're the one who has to live with the do.

If you're bored with your style but not ready to take the plunge and get it chopped, there are some more minor changes you can make for a little variety. Try parting your hair on the opposite side one day. Or see what you look like in a loose bun, or braids, or a headband, or clips. You can also try non-permanent dyes and streaks—these typically wash out in a few shampoos.

Hair is a great area for experimentation. Even the worst haircut or color will grow out. And you might just find a new style that makes you look—and feel—beautiful.

experimenting with
makeup

Right now, you'd probably love to get mistaken for someone a year or two older, and makeup seems like a pretty good way to do that. But are you even allowed to wear the stuff? Lots of parents have strict rules about it, and contrary to what you might think, it's not just to make your life difficult. Sure, part of it is that they don't want you to grow up too quickly (which they're going to have to get over pretty soon). But another part is that they know this is the time in your life when your skin is beautiful and smooth, your cheeks naturally rosy, your eyes sparkling, and your lashes full and long—all on their own! Older women envy your youthful glow, and at the risk of sounding just like your mom—you really don't need makeup!

But, okay, no one can deny that trying the stuff out is just plain fun, not to mention a big help on those mornings when you wake up with Mount Everest on your nose. The most important thing is that you feel

good about yourself, so if makeup gives you more confidence, then go for it. Just try to stick to a natural look that won't seem strange or garish on someone your age. Try using tinted moisturizer instead of heavy foundation, wearing shiny lip-gloss instead of lipstick, and curling your lashes with an eyelash curler instead of using clumpy mascara. Or if you want to go truly au naturel (or if you've got one of those strict parents mentioned above), just pinch your cheeks or gently bite your lips for a little extra color before heading into the class you share with your crush. For a date or a school dance, you can try laying it on a bit thicker. Enlist your mom, sister, or girlfriends to make you over before the big event. (For some tips and tricks, see pages 30–31.) However, your makeup is a reflection of your personality, so don't automatically copy exactly what everyone else does when something else might suit you much better.

Finally, don't forget the little detail that could spoil everything: ragged, bitten nails. To get your digits in hand-holding shape, think about picking up one of the special polishes made with a bitter taste to help you stop nibbling. Unfortunately, though, these don't work for everyone. The only real cure is for you to decide to quit. Tell your friends you're trying to cut back, and get them to help by nudging you when you unconsciously start biting. It's just a matter of willpower!

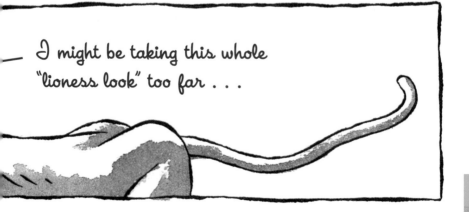

I might be taking this whole "lioness look" too far . . .

ph1

29

complexion

You can even out your complexion with tinted moisturizers or very light foundations. Choose the color when it's daylight outside, and try getting sample sizes until you find the perfect shade. Shades with yellow undertones suit most skin colors, from fair to dark. Pink undertones may work best for some olive complexions, though. Note that the right foundation will seem to disappear into your skin when you rub it on.

If you are using foundation, a little light blush will actually make you look less made up. Smile into your mirror when you apply it so it goes right onto the apples of your cheeks.

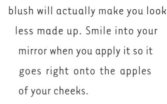

long, oval, or triangular face

Apply blush in a triangle on the cheeks, from the nose toward the temples.

round face

Apply blush in a triangle from the mouth toward the temples.

the mouth

Save bright reds for evening only. During the day, use pinker, more transparent colors, or shades of orange-brown. Don't try to "fix" your mouth if you think it's too thin by overdrawing a little—lipstick has a tendency to smear, and you don't want to end up looking like a clown! To make lipstick hold, apply a first coat, pat your lips with a paper tissue, then apply another layer, or buy a brand that's labeled "long-lasting" or "won't kiss off."

ph1

30

the eyes

There's an eye shadow for every color in the rainbow. But be careful: some colors don't look good on everyone! Cream shadows are transparent and iridescent. They can be very pretty, but can fade as the day goes by, or clump into the folds of the eyelids. Powdered shadows have good staying power, but are more striking.

choosing a good eye-makeup color (shadow or liner)

Blue eyes: blue and gray
Green eyes: mauve, green, brown
Hazel or brown eyes: mauve, green, brown, charcoal gray

round eyes

If you have round eyes and want to make them appear wider, extend eyeliner out past the outer corners. This works well for making small eyes seem larger, too.

applying eyeliner

Eyeliner can make your eyes look very dramatic. For daytime, you might just draw a line of color along your lower lid, as close to your lash line as possible *without* drawing inside the lid (getting makeup in your eye can cause irritation and infection). For nighttime, create dramatic '50s-style eyes by drawing a line of color on your upper lid, too. You may want to run your finger across it for a softer, smoky look.

wide-set eyes

If your eyes are set far apart and you want them to look as if they are closer together, apply eyeliner so it is thicker in the inner corner of your eye and thinner at the outer corner.

almond eyes

If you have almond eyes (like a cat's), you can accentuate their individuality by making them seem wider using the technique for round eyes.

look good, even when you're
dressing down

Your mom just doesn't appreciate your beautifully—purposefully—aged, ragged jeans. But they're your uniform—what makes you fit in with the fashionistas and, more importantly, feel good about the way look. Style is subjective, and you certainly don't want your parents picking out your clothes for you. So anything goes, as long as it suits you. Just don't stick to dingy jeans and baggy T-shirts if you're doing it to disappear into the crowd or to hide your new figure. At some point you'll realize you look your best when you use your sense of style to stand out, and you'll regret covering up your true self for so long.

If you're stuck in a rut, break out of it by taking little fashion risks. It's often the details that make all the difference, so start by trying new accessories and jewelry, something you wouldn't normally wear. Hats are big right now, and there are lots of cute (and cheap) ones to choose from. For your own secret fun, wear cute underwear with funky designs—you'll be the only one who knows, but it'll give you a little extra confidence boost nonetheless!

Don't forget to pay attention to your shoes. The rule is simple: not too big, not too small, not too flat, not too tall. Your spinal column and your knees will suffer if you're teetering around in uncomfortable shoes. Of course, on special occasions you can wear heels. But try to stick with flats (the non-platform kind, preferably) for everyday.

If you haven't already, chances are you'll want to pierce your ears—or some other body part!—at some point. (You'll probably need your parents' permission while you're under eighteen.) Be sure to get it done at a reputable place—that is, not in your best friend's bathroom with a sewing needle and some ice, and maybe not at Dirty Harry's Roadside Tattoo Palace either. Department stores and accessories shops are a pretty safe bet. Once it's done, follow the care instructions you're given to the letter—that likely means cleaning with rubbing alcohol daily and not taking out the piercing studs for several weeks. If you're careless about piercings, they can become infected and cause a lot of pain.

your glasses

Put your glasses on when you watch TV. Put your glasses on to do your homework. Wear your glasses in class. You're really starting to hate your glasses! But for now, you need them. Besides, glasses can make you look very smart, sophisticated, and sexy! There are many cute frame shapes and colors to choose from, so your glasses can be just one more awesome accessory.

Your vision won't stabilize until you're a bit older—it may get worse or get better. That's why you have to keep a close watch on its development; your health is at stake. If you have headaches, for example, it may mean you're not seeing clearly and you need a new prescription. The wrong prescription might cause other symptoms as well, such as losing your balance or bumping into things a little more often than you should.

As for getting contacts, they can be a big responsibility. You have to remember when to take them out and how to clean them properly in order to avoid infection. But if you think you're ready, bring the topic up with your parents and explain why you think you're capable of taking care of them. In the future, you can also think about getting laser vision-correction surgery, but you'll have to wait till you're over eighteen, when your vision is less likely to change.

Of course I can't see anything, but I'm the only one who wears them like this!

too tall, too short,

IT'S UNIVERSAL: no teenage girl is completely happy with her body. Every girl can find some part to obsess over. Rest assured that the imperfections you notice on yourself are probably not visible to anyone but you. (Everyone else is too busy worrying about her own body to notice what's supposedly "wrong" with yours!) There are some things you just can't change. Your height is one of them—so you might as well learn to look on the bright side. If you are short, you have options: you can be your height when you want to or wear cool heels when you want a few extra inches. If you are tall, you have a serious shopping advantage—so many fashions look great on tall folks.

If feeling like being too skinny is your problem, you should count your blessings. When you reach adulthood you'll probably have fewer health problems than larger women. Besides, in time, you're likely to gain the weight your body is meant to, albeit slowly.

too skinny,

too fat

IF, ON THE OTHER HAND, you think you're overweight, begin by asking yourself this question: Am I the only one who thinks I'm too big, or would others—like my mother or my doctor—agree? The extra pounds may only exist in your head. And believing that you're fat when you're actually not can lead to dangerous eating disorders. Girls with a disorder called anorexia nervosa starve themselves, refusing to eat in order to compulsively lose weight, even when they get down as low as eighty pounds. Girls with a related disorder called bulimia eat normal-to-large amounts, then force themselves to vomit in order to lose weight. These are very serious psychological problems that are harmful to your health, and can be fatal. If you suffer from this kind of behavior, you should confide in an adult you trust and see a doctor immediately.

If you've seen a doctor and have confirmed that you are, in fact, overweight, there are things you can do to improve your health and your appearance. First off, don't be tricked into trying fad diets or pills or products that promise to melt away pounds practically overnight. There's no easy fix for becoming fit, and after using these methods, you're likely to gain back any weight that you've lost. (Plus, some of these diet products can actually do your body a lot of harm.) Instead, the best way to get in shape is through exercise and healthy eating; your goal is to adopt healthy habits that you can maintain for the rest of your life. So rather than going crazy and cutting out all your favorite foods, take baby steps: a little less sugar, whole-wheat bread instead of white, fruits and veggies instead of french fries. Find a type of exercise that you enjoy and a friend to do it with—you're much likelier to get into a routine if you're doing something fun.

It's much easier to maintain a healthy weight than to have to lose a whole lot after you've gained it. So whether or not you're in shape right now, start getting into the habit of eating good-for-you foods, and you'll be very happy you did down the road.

Cracking open cans of spinac

ph1

38

eat your spinach!

A good diet is balanced and varied. You have to eat a little bit of everything: vegetables for vitamins, fish for phosphorus and healthy types of fat, low-fat dairy for calcium, and lean meat or eggs for protein. You have to be sure not to eat the same thing every day. Force yourself every now and then to eat the things you don't like very much. And if, truly, you can only stand to eat hamburgers with french fries, or pizza, it's better to eat pizza . . . with some veggie toppings!

Cookies and candy and fast food will make you gain weight and, what's more, make your body produce cholesterol (a substance in the blood, too much of which can cause a heart attack!).

If you can't stand eating fruit, drink it in a smoothie instead. If you don't want to eat meat, eat nuts or eggs, which contain protein. If you don't like seafood, try tuna and salmon—they're less "fishy" than other fish.

...akes girls pretty, too!

If you're tired all the time, or your schoolwork is terrible and you always feel sleepy, you may not be getting enough iron. Iron is essential to the proper functioning of your brain. When you don't get enough, you may start to feel woozy. To remedy this, just add more iron to your diet! Find it in fortified cereals, soybeans, beef, chicken, broccoli, peas, lima beans, and kale.

As for the spinach your parents are always trying to get you to swallow, it doesn't actually have much iron. But it does have a decent amount of calcium.

If chocolate is your weakness, you don't have to feel too guilty eating it. Just make sure to get good-quality kinds with a higher percentage of cocoa, since they contain less sugar. Dark chocolate and, to a lesser extent milk chocolate, also contain substances called flavonols, which may protect against cancer and heart disease. And then there's the magnesium in chocolate, which is also good for your body. Just don't

overdo it—chocolate still has a lot of calories, so stick to one small square a day.

Don't forget to drink lots of water throughout the day. It's very important to stay hydrated. You may know the old rule, "Drink eight eight-ounce glasses of water a day." The truth is you'll get much of the liquid you need from food (broccoli is 90 percent water) and other beverages, so you don't need to be obsessive about the "8 x 8" rule. But drinking several glasses of water a day is definitely a good idea. Trying carrying a little bottle of water in your backpack. That way you'll always have it with you, and you'll remember to drink it.

Finally, try to eat three small meals and several small snacks every day. Breakfast is super-important: it gets your body working in the morning, and will keep you from bingeing at lunch later on. So don't skip it!

breathe deeply

Exercise makes you lose weight. It also shapes your body, makes it more muscular, and keeps it healthy. That's why it's absolutely necessary. But exercise doesn't just mean running on a treadmill at the gym. You can play a team sport like soccer, basketball, or field hockey. Or you can take a dance class, go swimming, or walk around your neighborhood. You can do indoor activities like gymnastics or aerobics, or

outdoor activities like hiking or tennis. Starting off slowly and then gradually increasing the duration and intensity of your exercise sessions will help you build muscles and burn calories safely.

If you want to join a health club, ask for an orientation or introduction to the machines and how they work. Exercise equipment can be dangerous if used incorrectly. Remember to

I love exercizzzz . . . zzzz . . . zzzzz

drink lots of water while you work out, and don't forget to breathe. It's best to exhale, or breathe out, while you're doing the hard part of the exercise (for example, while pushing the weight upward on a bench press).

The most important thing is to have fun and not to overdo it when you first start out. Be sensible and know your limitations. What's fine and good for your running partner isn't necessarily good for you. (If you have asthma, or any other health condition, it's important to consult your doctor before starting up an exercise routine.) Be aware of the weather—on super-hot summer days, you're more susceptible to heat exhaustion, so avoid working out outdoors during the middle of the day, when it's the sunniest. And if you ever feel light-headed or sick during exercise, end your session immediately.

There are three parts of your body you might not think to exercise, but they can certainly benefit from some conditioning. Don't forget to breathe while you do each move.

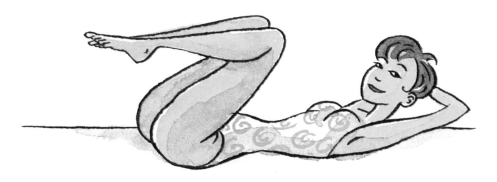

the abdominals

Working the abdominal muscles not only helps give you a flat stomach, it also helps support your back.

Lying on your back with your hands behind your head, bring your knees to your chest and then lower your legs to the floor while you breathe out, ten times in a row. Try alternating each leg, then doing both legs together. You should feel your abdominal muscles contract. It's critical that your back remain glued to the floor. If you feel it rise up, don't lower your legs as far. Do this exercise over again with your head and chest raised, looking at the ceiling. Vary it by raising your chest to meet your knees.

the knees

Joints are important. Your knees carry a lot of weight, and sports can put even more pressure on them. This exercise will strengthen the muscles around your knee, giving it more support. Sit down with your back to a wall with one leg stretched out, the other bent. Raise the straight leg, keeping it straight the whole time. Hold it for ten seconds and then lower it. Slowly raise it up and then down again, ten times. Now raise it, rotate it to one side, and hold for ten seconds. Then rotate it to the other side and hold it. Now rotate the leg from side to side ten times. Change legs and do the same. The straighter and closer to the wall your back is, the harder the exercise.

the bust

It's good to exercise the muscles that support your breasts—these muscles form sort of a natural bra. Lie on your back with your knees folded to glue your back to the ground. Use dumbbells that weigh a pound or two. Start with your arms spread wide, raise them straight up into the air above your chest. Hold for ten seconds, then lower again. Raise and lower them ten times.

Once again I had a terrible night. Somethin

get a good night's
sleep

Sleep is absolutely vital—which is perfect, because it feels great, too! Most people need a minimum of eight hours to function normally the next day. Preteens and teenagers should get even more sleep. It's really not good to stay up until midnight on a school night. So if there's a show you must see, tape it instead of letting it ruin your rest. And if you watch a horror movie right before bed, don't be surprised if you have nightmares.

If you sometimes have insomnia (that is, you can't fall asleep), think about what could be causing it. You might be stressed out by something like a test, a fight with your friends, or the crush you can't stop thinking about. Some tricks to combat insomnia: Don't eat a huge

don't know what, kept me away from my bed.

meal or exercise right before bedtime. Go to bed and wake up at the same time every day so your body gets into a routine. And don't keep looking at the clock; it'll only make you more anxious.

One last warning: don't take sleeping pills from your parents' medicine cabinet, or from anywhere else for that matter. They weren't prescribed for you, and aren't formulated for young people. Taking someone else's pills can be extremely dangerous.

smile!

Sometimes it's hard to accept yourself as you are. It's even harder now, when your body's changing so dramatically. But try to be patient through all of this. Respect your body, respect yourself—and others will respect you, too.

ph1

47

phase 2

get a hold
of yourself

ME FIRST!

you're one of a kind

I'M BORED
YOU'RE BORED
WE'RE ALL BORED

WHAT TYPE OF GIRL ARE YOU?

the art of laziness

NEED AIR? HOW TO GET RID OF YOUR FAMILY

me, me, me

Sometimes you look at yourself in the mirror and think, *Why am I such a nothing?* This kind of questioning usually comes after an especially bad encounter with someone: a teacher who has it in for you, a friend you feel like you don't measure up to, a boy who says something mean to you—or worse, ignores you. It can be pretty depressing. To cheer yourself up, there's only one thing to do: remind yourself that if everyone were exactly the same, the earth would be a pretty boring place. We all have little flaws, but we can learn to turn them to our advantage.

Take a girl who's really shy. She might turn out to be the most loyal, trusted friend, since she's so good at listening, while a girl who's always the life of the party might be too busy entertaining to lend an ear to a friend who needs to talk. A pessimist might pack an umbrella and rain gear on a beach vacation just assuming there'll be terrible weather . . . and be right, while an optimist might head off totally unprepared, thinking the weatherman must be exaggerating . . . and be right. Hooray for faults! Just for fun, see if you recognize yourself among any of the following character descriptions. (Hint: most people have bits of a few different types inside them.)

the pal

With you, everything's easy. You laugh at jokes, even if they're aimed at you. You're always ready to play Monopoly with your little brothers and sisters, and always set the table without having to be asked. Even if you're not a great scholar, your attitude makes your teachers love you. And you're always there for your friends whenever they need you. So just how do you manage all that? Simple: you've got a heart of gold. The only problem is that you can't bear to let others down—whatever they want, you deliver. So you sometimes have trouble saying no. And on the rare occasion that you happen to be in a bad mood, no one can understand it. They think someone as nice and kind and happy-go-lucky as you never has a bad day. But they're wrong! You have just as much right as anyone else to be disagreeable for a few minutes. The good thing with you is that it usually doesn't last much longer than a few minutes. And then you're back off again with a smile on your face.

ph2

51

So what do you think, is it me?

the comedian

No one ever complains that they're bored when you're around. You always have a joke to make everyone laugh—an inexhaustible supply of tricks. Only sometimes your tendency to play around gets you into sticky situations. Like when you've disrupted class for the fifteenth time with one of your brilliant and clever quips. The result: you've gotten a reputation for being the class clown. Sometimes you get tired of always playing tricks, but now that everyone expects them from you, you feel like you have to keep 'em coming. But the truth is that you can tone it down when necessary. By always trying to make people laugh, you might be forgetting to listen to what they have to say. So try to find a good balance between the two.

ph2

the **chatterbox**

You have more than a few traits in common with the comedian, although strangely enough, you don't always get along well with her. You have to take center stage, and so does she. So you really shine when you're hanging out with a group of quieter people. You always have a story to tell, but be careful—since you spend so much time talking, you sometimes end up repeating yourself for lack of new material. There's nothing worse than hearing, "Yeah, you already told us that!" And if you really overdo it, people might stop paying attention altogether. Like the comedian, you're usually fun to be around because you provide the entertainment. But if you were a better listener once in a while, your friends might have the chance to tell you their interesting stories.

the straight-talker

Someone forgot to tell you: total honesty is not always the best policy! But, to you, it feels like your duty. If your friend's new haircut resembles that of a well-groomed poodle, you tell her, sincerely believing you're doing her a favor. You don't sugar-coat anything for anyone. Not that that's an entirely bad thing, though. You opinion is often sought after, because people trust you to tell it like it is. Still, if you could learn to be more tactful, you might offend fewer of your classmates. There are ways to be truthful and still be nice about it.

miss curious

Curious types often make great listeners; you're always genuinely interested in what other people are saying, so you ask lots of questions to find out the full story. If you're inquisitive and discreet, you're someone people will want to confide in (even though you're pretty good at worming their secrets out of them!). You know how to give good advice, and your friends know they can trust you.

Those who are curious but not discreet, however, aren't always so popular. If you'll tell everything you know in order to be let in on more gossip, your friends will soon realize that you can't keep a secret, and they'll stop confiding theirs. Try to remember that people deserve a little privacy—after all, aren't there things that you would prefer the whole school not find out? You'll make a lot more friends (and fewer enemies) by keeping someone's secrets rather than sharing them.

the girl scout

You don't give yourself or your friends a moment's rest. You could never just sit around gossiping while there are important things to be done! Whether it's planning the next student council meeting or collecting school supplies to send to children in developing countries, you're always busy. You're willing to sacrifice your own free time to help others—and you expect your friends to do the same. Unfortunately, you sometimes wear them out, harassing them to sign your petition against discrimination or to donate food for the homeless. They usually let it go because you are, after all, a good friend. But you might all be a little happier if you occasionally take time to breathe. Choose the causes you think are especially worth fighting for: it's better to devote yourself fully to one thing than to spread yourself too thin.

the scaredy-cat

People always say that you're shy, quiet, and introverted. The truth is, you don't have much self-confidence. If your best friend happens to resemble one of the types mentioned earlier, you probably never get a word in edgewise! And that's often why stronger personalities get along best with you: you never say no, you're afraid to disagree, and you tend to just go along with whatever they say. You never raise your hand in class, even when you know the answer. Above all, you don't want to be noticed. But the thing is, if you loosened up a little and let your true self show through, lots of people would find you great company! You've observed a lot from your quiet corner—share some of what you've seen and figured out. Speak up! Get involved! You've got nothing to lose and the world has everything to gain.

the eccentric

You truly are one of a kind. You love the daring and the unusual, which could make you really well-suited for a cool and creative career in the future. Your room is cluttered and full of all the interesting things you've amassed, from silver skull rings to Cherokee headdresses—to the delight of your friends and the despair of your mom! You're interested in everything. You would be a fountain of knowledge if you weren't also a little superficial, loving all things edgy and alternative just because they freak people out a little. With your ultra-unique style, you never go unnoticed, but that could mean potential friends and boyfriends watching in awe from afar, too intimidated to get any closer. Be you, but make sure others know that your originality doesn't mean you aren't warm, friendly, and approachable.

I don't like flowers, either!

HELIOT

never satisfied

Nothing's ever right to you. The mashed potatoes in the cafeteria don't have enough salt, or they have too much. Your math teacher is useless, your new jeans look too new, and your vacation was a catastrophe because it rained two out of the seven days. Okay, sure, most people would agree that those things are a bummer. But you feel the need to go on and on about them, complaining to anyone who will listen. Moaning about things might actually make you feel less miserable, but unfortunately, no one else really likes to hear it, and at some point, they'll get sick of it. (Which, on the bright side, would be something else for you to complain about!) But seriously: try a little harder to see the good side of life. Sure, rain makes your hair frizz out, but it also makes the flowers grow . . .

the dreamer

You've always got your head in the clouds, lost in your own imagination. You daydream about boys, about celebrities, about anything that pops into your head. You fantasize about being a supermodel or a figure-skating champion. Some people have built their lives around achieving their dreams, so go ahead and set your sights high! On the other hand, your friends (not to mention your teachers) are never quite sure where you are when you get that distant look. Don't lose sight of what's going on around you. Keep dream-  ing, but don't let that stop you from enjoying your real life right now.

Unfortunately, there is also a second type of dreamer: the compulsive liar. You say anything that comes into your head—whether or not it's actually true. For you, exaggerating the truth is a way of making yourself seem more interesting, or of living the life you wish you had. The trouble is that people won't treat you as a dreamer, but as a liar. It's like the story of the little boy who cried wolf: when you tell too many fibs, no one will believe you when you actually are being honest. So try to stick to the facts. Take advantage of your rich imagination by writing down your stories instead. Nobody ever accuses a novelist of being a liar!

ph2

59

i like myself, i hate myself

It's inevitable: you're going to have good days and bad days. If you're totally in love with yourself 24/7, you're either lying or you're crazy! And if seeing your reflection in the mirror makes you want to puke every single day, then you've got a serious self-image problem.

It's much more likely you're a pretty normal person, with normal highs and lows. This morning, you looked drop-dead gorgeous. No one could resist you! Tomorrow you'll be lamenting over that hideous pimple that popped up on your forehead overnight (they're often sneaky like that. . .). You'll try everything: a baseball cap, brushing your bangs down over your face, your sister's foundation makeup. Nothing works. Then you suddenly notice for the first time that your eyes are way too close-set. And is it just you, or does your nose grow bigger and bigger

ever day? That's it: you look like an idiot, and, according to your last grade in English, it's more than just looks. What's more, you don't have much of a sense of humor, since your big nose is depressing you all the time. No boy will ever want you. You won't get into college. And then, your father knocks on the bathroom door and says "Honey, of course you're pretty. Can I shave now?"

Time out. Take a deep breath and calm down. You know deep down it's not really that bad! You just need to get back into a better mood. Think about the day ahead of you—there must be something good coming up in the not-so-distant future. Your French class, maybe—you're good at it, and your teacher likes you. (If not French, than art. Or soccer practice. Or something!) And then after school you'll meet up with your best friends. You can tell them anything and they'll understand. They'll convince you that no one can even see your pimple, especially with the foundation, the bangs, and the cap. And if none of that succeeds in cheering you up, maybe it's the day to indulge in a double-thick milk-shake or to treat yourself to a new lipstick, or to haul out all your clothes and try on everything till you find something that makes you feel fabulous—anything that gives you that extra boost back to feeling like yourself again.

ph2

61

HÉLIOT

you're bored?
you're so lucky!

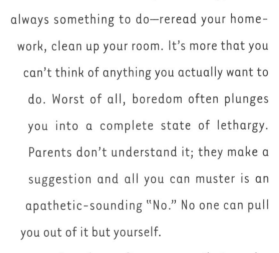

How many times have you sat around silently screaming, "I'm bored!" Boredom is sort of an illusion, since really, there's always something to do—reread your homework, clean up your room. It's more that you can't think of anything you actually want to do. Worst of all, boredom often plunges you into a complete state of lethargy. Parents don't understand it; they make a suggestion and all you can muster is an apathetic-sounding "No." No one can pull you out of it but yourself.

Boredom often means that you're ready for new things (or old things you may have forgotten . . .). So it's the ideal time to follow your curiosity. The best thing you can do for yourself is to get off the couch. Head outside. See how many times you can bounce a ball off the side of the house and catch it. Walk around the block. Walk through the woods. Walk to a friend's house. If you're stuck inside, try the oldest trick in the book: looking through the bookshelf! Okay, so you probably don't have the slightest desire to read. Doesn't matter. Just open a few books, read a couple lines at random, pull your choices out, and put off reading until you actually feel like it. Or, try taking a look at the atlas (you might find one in your parents' car.) Look at the world, the states and the countries, the names of the capitals. It's like traveling in your head. Make a mental list of all  the places you want to visit in your life. Or, peek at your mother's recipes in the kitchen. You never know, you might have a sudden urge to whip up a peach pie! Cooking is a great way to get rid of boredom and please other people with your treats. As a last resort, look at the TV guide and make a list of all the interesting shows during the week—but only the ones on weird channels that you don't normally watch.

If you can, find a friend to be bored with. Once you're together, anything's possible. Do what you never do: Go to a museum. Go to the record store and listen to different music than you usually listen to. You're bound to make more than a few discoveries. This might even be a good time to try meeting new people other than those you normally hang out with (after all, you might be bored because your friends are all busy). So think about calling up someone new. Who knows . . . someone you've only talked to in class up till now might turn into a super-close friend.

ph2

64

passion is your
best friend

And it's the best cure for boredom. If you have something you're passionate about, you're one of the lucky ones—it can take some time to find an activity or hobby or cause that you care deeply about. No one's passion is any better or more noble than anyone else's; all that matters is that getting involved in it makes you happy. You play the piano? Cool. You collect stamps? Perfect. You love French cinema? Great! Even if your passion is assembling the world's longest paper-clip chain . . . why not? Really great collections can actually become valuable over the years (although you might have more luck with, say, concert memorabilia than paper clips!). You can have several passions at the same time, too—that's even better.

And to think, nobody realizes what a colossal effort I'm making right now . . .

an underappreciated
virtue

Still sitting around doing nothing? People might call you lazy, but they don't realize just how important a little rest and relaxation can be. Someone who's "lazy" takes the time to breathe. She knows the good things in life, and appreciates each one of those little moments in which she does . . . nothing. And it's got nothing to do with boredom. Someone who knows how to be lazy has the time to fill her head full of interesting things. And contrary to what you might think, a lazybones is often a good worker. Where other people take two hours to do something, a lazy girl will only take one. Why? Because her brain keeps working during her moments of laziness. She's also perfectly organized, even though you couldn't tell by looking at her desk or her room. Working well and working quickly (so you don't have to do things over again), means you've got more time to be lazy. And to be lazy is to . . .

. . . dream

It's important not to confuse the true dreamers and the occasional dreamers. We've already talked about the first (see page 59). Occasional dreamers have their feet on the ground at all times, even if they do sometimes have their head in the clouds. We know that playing helps babies develop their intelligence. Well, dreaming is a way of playing in your head when you're too old for Thomas the Tank Engine and Barbie dolls. It's good to dream. Dreaming develops your imagination, your creativity, and your new ideas. Great thinkers and artists are first and foremost great dreamers. So there's absolutely no risk in getting lost in your dreams, so long as you remember that they're only dreams. That doesn't prevent you from expressing them in stories and paintings and through other creative outlets.

You can also write poetry,

or keep a journal. It might seem old-fashioned, but lots of people swear by it. It lets you get out all your private thoughts and emotions, so they don't stay bottled up inside, or come exploding out at your friends or parents. In adolescence, boys turn more to sports or to other group activities to express themselves, while many girls turn more inward and give priority to exploring what's inside. Of course, that doesn't mean girls don't also play sports! And the truth is, boys may also write poems . . . most of them just don't dare admit it.

secret feelings

Some of what you write in your journal will probably have a lot do with your feelings about growing up. For example, maybe you secretly still love playing with your dolls. You can't resist saying "goo-goo, ga-ga" to the neighbor's baby. You bring home stray animals to care for, much to your parents' dismay, and you never tire of brushing and grooming your cat. You dream about being a teacher or a pediatrician or a social worker. All this points to a strong maternal instinct—you love caring for those who need you.

On the other hand, maybe all you think about is who's going to win the World Cup. You love beating the boys at basketball. Your dream is to explore the Amazon rainforest in a canoe. Your sister and her dumb lacy dresses drive you crazy. If that's all true for you, sounds like you're a tomboy—although that's kind of an outdated term, since lots of girls are into sports and other stuff that used to be only for boys back in the old days. Nonetheless, being a girl might seem like kind of a nuisance to you right now. You don't want to change into a woman. You want to stay on equal footing with boys, like before . . . before your body changed without bothering to ask whether you wanted it to or not. Rest assured that you can still be just as good as the guys. And if it's bothering you that boys are starting to look at you differently—you know, like a girl—you'll realize soon enough that there is an upside to that after all.

all alone!

The most important thing to a two-year-old is setting off on her own for the first time: toddling away from Mom and Dad, getting into things she's not supposed to—all that fun stuff. As she gets older, this urge sort of fades a little. But, then, right around the age you are now, it comes back with a vengeance.

Suddenly, you'd rather die than do anything with your parents in tow. You want to go to the movies alone, to parties alone, to the beach alone. And by "alone," you don't actually mean you, by yourself, with no one else. You mean without your parents. Of course, this desire to be rid of them quickly evaporates the minute you need a skirt hemmed or your favorite jeans washed before Friday night. But the thing is, if you want to be treated like an adult, you have to accept the inconveniences that

Anything I can help you with, Dad? Want me to help you watch that?

go along with the benefits. We know—you've heard that before! But accepting it can really work to your advantage. Prove to your parents that you can take care of yourself and they might actually let you. Make your bed and vacuum your room without being asked. Don't beg your mom nonstop to sew this or wash that—instead, ask her to show you how to do it and then do it yourself from now on. She'll appreciate your efforts and be more inclined to say yes the next time you ask to do something on your own (although you might have to remind her how responsible you've been lately when you make your request). Besides, when you're doing your own laundry, you'll always have what you need exactly when you need it—no more relying on mom's housecleaning schedule. And doesn't it drive you crazy when people come and rifle through your things with the excuse of cleaning? If you keep your room neat on your own, it'll never happen again. Speaking of things that annoy you, how about eating that gross casserole your Dad always makes for dinner? Help out by making the family dinner yourself and you can have whatever you want. A little autonomy can go a long way.

you're somebody

To be autonomous is to be self-assured. It involves all the little things in everyday life that we slowly learn to master. But it also means having confidence in yourself. It means that what other people think of you is not what's most important to you. It's up to you to grow up inside your head and become autonomous. Independence isn't just a matter of earning your own pocket-money (which you can do, of course, by looking for a babysitting job, or helping neighbors do yard work). Being independent means having your own ideas and opinions and being able to defend them. You aren't just Ms. Crandall's daughter or Joanne's little sister. You are a unique individual with her own name and her own personality. So make a name for yourself.

get organized . . .

Does this sound like a typical day for you? You realize two minutes before school that you forgot to do your English homework. You were supposed to buy a new notebook for it, but you don't have a penny in your purse. You can't call a friend to see how she did the assignment because you can't find her number. Now you're running late because you can't find the shirt that goes with these pants anywhere. And to top it all off, you just remembered that you wanted to tape *Friends* last night, but it totally slipped your mind. You have a serious problem: you've got to get organized! It sounds like a pain, but it can save you precious time and make your life a lot easier.

Isn't it frustrating to be constantly running around looking for something? If you're tired of having a million-and-one of these little crises every day, get in the habit of following a few very simple rules. Use a planner, and write down everything you want to remember in it, from the math project due next week to the season premiere of your favorite show. Do your homework right away instead of putting it off. Would you rather spend your free time with the nagging thought of homework in the back of your head, or just relaxing and enjoying yourself, knowing that all your obligations are taken care of? Keep your work in labeled binders or notebooks. That way you'll never lose anything important. If you want to be sure not to miss something important, put Post-Its on your mirror or your dresser—somewhere you'll be sure to see

them (and don't forget to take down old notes once you don't need them anymore). Keep a budget. If you're lucky enough to get a regular allowance, divide the amount between what you need (school supplies, bus pass, new gloves . . .) and what you want (candy, T-shirts, video games . . .). The first category has priority, since it might be required by your parents, otherwise they'll stop giving you allowance. If you only come into money from time to time, think seriously before you spend it. You don't want to regret wasting it on little things you don't really need the day the CD you've been dying for goes on sale.

on your own . . .

There are actually times when it's your parents who are pushing you to spend time away from them. OK, so it's usually to do things that aren't much fun, like grocery shopping or visiting Aunt Bertha. But then, there are the golden opportunities to go off without them for something you really want to do, like a class trip. Do everything you can to persuade your parents to let you go alone. (Your arguments: it's educational, there'll be teachers to keep an eye on us, it's good exercise, I'll help pay. . .).

Worried that your teachers will be just like surrogate parents? Contrary to what you might think, they're usually a lot cooler on field trips than they are in class. Take advantage of the more relaxed setting to form better relationships with them—it might pay off back at school, and on your report card! Just don't wander off and get lost during the day, or sneak out to the boys' rooms at night (or both!). And obviously the real draw to a class trip is bonding with your friends—you'll be remembering these trips for years to come.

Then there are the camps parents might ship you off to during summer vacation. They're not children's camps any more (you're too old), but you still have the feeling that they're trying to get rid of you. But who cares! You could use a break from them, too, and camp can be more fun than you've ever had before. You might be a little nervous to go off alone, but believe us, you won't be lonely for long. Between the activities, the new friends—and the new boys!—you'll never want to go back home. You can choose a camp that corresponds to one of your passions (art camp, theatre camp, horseback-riding camp), or you can try something entirely different if you're looking to get out of a rut.

The ultimate opportunity to go off on your own? Participating in a foreign-exchange program. The advantage: you're still living with a family, even if it is someone else's! The disadvantage: you don't know which family you'll end up with. But the organizations that run these programs will try to pick the best people to place you with. Obviously, you'll have to learn another language. But cavorting around Europe or South America or wherever like a local is definitely worth it!

want to have some fun?

ME AND EV

ARE ALL GUYS DOGS?

IT'S NOT SO EASY TALKING TO BOYS . . .

break out of
your shell

like yourself
and others will
like you . . .

ERYONE ELSE

but a little effort
WILL CHANGE THAT

people are strange

Since there's not much chance that you'll get to live as a hermit on the top of a mountain with only sheep for company, you have to learn to live in harmony with other people. Often you're happy to have them around. But then there are days that make you long for the sheep. Human beings are social animals, and most of the time that's a good thing. There are some days when being a part of your family is great, and others when you think you must be adopted. So how do you deal? Try a little bit of diplomacy.

dad

Daddy and his little girl can be an unbeatable pair. Some fathers refuse their beloved daughters (almost) nothing. If your father's like this, count your blessings! He'll always be there for you, no matter what. So don't act like a little baby who has a tantrum if she's not allowed to have candy before dinner. You're just too old for that. Show him how much you love and appreciate him. And if you happen to be especially affectionate with him before asking him for money, it couldn't hurt! On the other hand, if your father isn't the type to give in easily . . . surprise him with a big hug—he won't be able to resist. With any type of dad, you have to realize that he's probably a little scared to see his

When did you get so big?

baby girl growing up. He misses the time when your hair was in pigtails and your face was covered in chocolate. Then he knew what to do—wash, diaper, feed, nap. Now he doesn't have a clue! So don't make it any harder on him. Talk to him about his work, or movies or art or politics or sports. Ask him for advice. And if he's hesitant to let you do the things you want to do, explain to him that you're older and more responsible now, and that you know how to take care of yourself and stay safe, even when you're doing grown-up things.

mom

Your mom knows what it's like to be a girl. She's gone through what you're going through right now, and that can make the two of you closer than anyone else—if you let her in. If you tell her when you get your first period, she'll gladly explain the best ways to deal with it. If you tell her when your crush breaks your heart, she can get you through it with some Ben & Jerry's and Kleenex. Of course, your mom isn't one of your girlfriends, and there'll be things you'd rather she didn't know. But then again, because she's not a friend, you can be more open with her without worrying what she'll think—she'll always love you no matter what. So confide in her from time to time—she'll be flattered that you came to her. When you want a favor from her, explain yourself calmly,

Great new haircut, Mom.

away from the rest of the family. Choose the right time. If she's dealing with your misbehaving little brother, for example, you'll only irritate her more. Try approaching her in the kitchen. While she's making dinner, set the table or offer to chop carrots or something, and talk while you work. She'll appreciate the help and talking will provide extra entertainment during a normally mundane chore—so you start off on her good side right away. That's diplomacy, and it works! The car is another good place. Long drives are especially great for discussing difficult issues— you don't even have to look each other in the eye, since you'll be paying attention to the road.

Prepare your arguments so you're not caught off-guard. If she sticks to her guns, try to understand her reasons instead of just getting mad. Then allow some time to pass and try her one more time. She might just reconsider when she sees how important your request is to you.

By the way, can I go out tonight?

older brothers

Your older brothers' and sisters' attitudes toward you have pretty much always been some version of "Leave me alone!" But now that you're a preteen or teenager, you realize they had their reasons. And as you get older, you and your siblings actually have a chance to be more like friends than enemies.

Your big brother might be a little disconcerted (maybe even more than Dad) that you're starting to wear makeup and have boyfriends and have a life of your own. He was used to seeing you running to the bathroom in your underpants in the morning. Now you head in there early and stay for hours. But your big brother can be a useful ally. He'll be protective of you if you ever get picked on, or if some dumb guy treats you badly. And . . . he's got lots of friends! What could be better than your own built-in, preapproved dating pool! Just be careful how you approach him for favors. Try not to whine or bug him. And consider getting him into a good mood first by letting him beat you at video games. Then say something like, "Can you help me? You're bigger/stronger/older/wiser. And I know people listen to you and respect you." Don't ask him for too much too often; he'll be more likely to help if you only ask when it's really important.

Your big sister, on the other hand, won't be surprised by your new behavior. She might even lecture you on the finer points of adolescence, or try to make you her personal project. This might drive you crazy, but

then again, she might throw some pretty good advice your way. Tell her your secrets, and she'll tell you hers. Ask her for her opinion from time to time and she'll be flattered—and maybe more likely to share clothes and bathroom space with you.

Just don't butt in when she has friends over. (But invite her to hang out sometimes when yours are there. She might get a kick out of offering her seasoned perspective to everyone.) Little by little, she'll accept you into her world, maybe even taking you when she goes out at night (all the while complaining, of course, about having to bring along her kid sister!). If you aren't always tugging at her sleeve to pay attention to you, just chilling out quietly instead and not hogging the conversation, she'll appreciate your company.

Sometimes it seems impossible to communicate with your brothers and sisters. Everything just winds up turning into an argument. But diplomacy really can work wonders. Even if your siblings fly into a rage, don't get sucked in. (They might be older, but you can be the more mature one!) Stay calm, rather than trying to scream louder than they do. It's less tiring and will yield better results, since they'll be a little taken aback by your approach. Yelling actually shows a lack of confidence: if you have good arguments, you don't need to get angry. So think first . . . scream later, if there really is no other solution.

younger brothers

With younger siblings, you can exercise your authority a bit. But be careful not to yell too much when they annoy you—your mom might intervene, and then you'll be the one paying for it. You probably get stuck with them a lot, because you're older and it's your job to take care of them when your parents need help. A lot of times it's a real pain, but once in a while, isn't it kind of fun to play hide-and-seek and leapfrog like you did when you were little? And if you're even just a little bit nice to little brothers and sisters, they'll idolize you. That doesn't mean you have to let them invade your space when you need some privacy. Just promise them that you'll play with them later or tomorrow if they'll stay out of your room while your friends are over. But it's important that you always keep these promises; they won't forget that you're

supposed to play in the sandbox or take them to see a movie. If you don't do it, they can make your life a living hell—by complaining to your parents, among other things. When it comes to little sibs, you're always the one in charge. So give them a little of your time and attention, but make them understand what the limits are.

and sisters

friends

What would life be without them? There's nothing better than having a bunch of girlfriends over to watch movies, paint each other's nails, and—of course—talk about guys! Many girls have a best friend, a few close friends, and a slew of acquaintances. It's sort of practical, since they can change and shift often: you have fights, you make up, you betray each other, and you forgive each other. Right now, your friendships might be a little unstable. You can't stand it if your

best friend spends time with a girl you don't like. You feel left out when two of your friends start shopping every day after school without you. These things might come up from time to time when you're older, but for the most part, as people grow up, they start to learn that true friendship is all about thoughtfulness and respect. You're sure to experience this kind of mature friendship as long as you follow a few simple rules. First off, try not to be a gossip; one day it'll come back to haunt you. As for joking around with your friends, you can tease gently, but there's no need to be mean. (Tip: Your friends will accept your sense of humor more readily if you make yourself the butt of the joke every now and then!) Next, a friend is someone who gives and receives. It's never just one or the other. So since she's there for you when you need to talk, you should be there for her, too.

Finally, understand that not all friendships are meant to last forever. You have some good times together, and sometimes that's all there is to it. By the end of the year you're hanging out with someone entirely different. It's not the end of the world—even though sometimes it might feel like it. When a friend breakup happens suddenly and violently, you might feel betrayed, hurt, or depressed. Just like in love, you don't

always get back what you put out into the relationship. On the other hand, your friendship might dissolve over time, and you realize one day that you just don't have much in common anymore. You've evolved in one direction, she's evolved in another. When this happens, it's normal to be a little sad. But then you just have to move on and make new friends that can relate more to the new you.

To develop a really lasting friendship, you have to try to banish envy and jealousy. If something good happens to your friend, you should be happy for her, and not say to yourself, "I wish it had happened to me and not her." And you shouldn't prevent her from going out with other people—you're both capable of having additional friends, and it doesn't mean you love each other any less. And with a really good friend, even if you don't see each other for days or weeks—or even months—you can still pick up where you left off. A true friend will never betray you. She will guard your secrets to the death. She will be by your side when you're in trouble. She will remember your birthday, come to your graduation, be your bridesmaid when you get married, and be godmother to your first baby. And you'll do the same for her.

what you shouldn't wish
on anyone

OK, so what if you don't have any friends? Nobody likes feeling lonely, but most people experience it at one time or another, even really popular girls. You might feel as if you're on the outside of a particular group—or all the groups. If that's the case, ask yourself why. Maybe it's because you're really shy, or a little too standoffish, or are just into different things than most of the kids you know. Is the situation your fault? Maybe, maybe not. But there's almost always something you can do to fix it.

Step one: finding someone else who's just like you. There must be at least one other girl in your class with the same problem as you—who, for whatever reason, can't seem to communicate with the other girls. If you're both super-introverted, take the initiative to strike up a conversation with her. If she's carrying a library book, ask her what she's reading. If you're both have the same boring teacher, commiserate with her about today's awful history lesson. Or, at the very least, just offer her a few M&Ms at lunch. Smiling more often couldn't hurt either—if you always sort of look like you're in a bad mood, it's possible people are a little intimidated by you. A simple kind word here or there could really open doors for you. If you've tried it all and rnothing works, rethink your strategy. Why not try to make friends outside of school? Join a town sports league where there'll be kids from different districts. Take a drawing class at a community college that's open to younger students. Or head off to camp for the summer—you're almost guaranteed a cabin full of new friends. Another option: get into social activism. Volunteer at a soup kitchen. Start a community-, church-, or school-based charity drive. Take up the cause against the slaughter of elephants in Africa (or whatever animal currently needs saving). Use your imagination. Whether or not it's exactly your fault that you don't have as many friends as you'd like, it's up to you to do something about it. If you don't, your loneliness will only continue. Just don't give up and say to yourself, "I don't care, I'm better off alone." It's not true. Everybody needs— and deserves—companionship.

On the other hand, if you happen to be someone with lots of friends, pay attention to the girls sitting alone in the cafeteria and walking around by themselves on school field trips. Ask them to come over and hang out with you. Even if they seem different from you at first, they might just be cool, interesting, amazing people inside. You just have to dig a little . . .

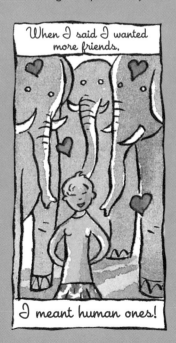

When I said I wanted more friends,

I meant human ones!

ph3

boys

Think about what happens when you accidentally make eye contact with a boy across the room—you laugh and blush bright red, right? When you were ten that never happened. Either you played with boys just like you'd play with girls and there was nothing to it, or you thought they had cooties and stayed as far away as possible. Now, it's as if there are two camps, staked out very close to each other, but nervous about visiting—the guys and the girls.

Of course you talk to each other, and do schoolwork together when you have to. But if you were to put five girls and five boys who don't know each other into the same room together, it wouldn't take three minutes before they'd form two totally separate groups, one on either side of the room. Gender relations are a little delicate right now, to say the least. Even though you're all the same age, the girls are a bit ahead of the boys in terms of maturity, both physically and mentally. In two or three years this difference will disappear. But, for the moment, boys seem dumb, vulgar, rough, and a little babyish. They don't seem to care about the same things you do—like who likes whom, and who's asking whom to the dance. But you should know: they're not as totally oblivious to girls as they seem. The physical changes you're going through are pretty interesting to them—as embarrassing as that is for you! Maybe

HELIOT

you overhear them discussing who's got the biggest bra size in class, or some similarly rude subject. Try to blow it off. They'll grow out of it soon enough. (Of course some guys never do, but you'll learn to stay away from those losers.)

For now, it's all about ignoring them. That'll keep you from losing your temper or bursting into tears. For better or worse, boys aren't very refined when they talk about girls. Although, neither are you when you talk about boys, but at least you're more discreet!

Of course, there are some boys you can tolerate—the nice ones who just seem to want to be friends. And it's good to have friends who are guys—so make things even easier for them. Help carry on the conversation: talk about schoolwork, music, or new movies. And just laugh off the comments the more obnoxious guys make. Let them know that you're not five anymore—you're way above their stupid behavior. Above all, don't be afraid to talk to boys—it's really not all that different from talking to girls. Pretty soon, it'll start to come naturally.

the mysteries of
charm

So when you find a boy who's actually way more cute than repulsive, how do you make him think the same about you? Charm is a tricky thing. People often think that you have to do something different to make yourself attractive: you have to wear lots of makeup so you seem older, or you have to act like you're too cool to care about stuff like getting good grades or trying out for drama club. But wearing bright red lipstick and acting aloof won't make a boy think you're someone you're not. And if it did, it wouldn't take him long to figure out his mistake! Be yourself, first and foremost. If you try to play the part of the girl you think he'll like, you'll be so ill at ease that you'll blow it altogether.

In fact, people are often at their most charming when they aren't trying. We're liked for things we're not even aware of. A sense of humor, a certain air of mystery, and interesting conversation are much more effective than mascara. You've probably spent many afternoons daydreaming about finding the great love of your life. Don't rush it—enjoy the dreaming for now. At this point, girls are more interested in romantic stuff than boys are, so give 'em a little time to catch up. If you're lucky enough to hold hands with a guy or get a quick smooch here and there—that's always exciting! But don't hurry into anything more serious. You're just at the beginning, and there'll be plenty of time for that down the road.

ph3

93

two great ways to get to know

guys

A lot of times, it's easier to meet guys when you're on vacation. You're more relaxed, and you're not being judged or observed by the other girls in your class. Okay, your parents are there, but they're not looking over your shoulder as much—often you can go out without them tagging along fifty paces behind you. Just don't forget that boys are

even shyer than you are. So be the one to strike up a conversation. At the beach, "accidentally" let the waves carry you over to where he's bodysurfing with his brother and ask if they're staying at the big hotel right on the shore, too. At the ski resort, take a lesson for your age group and ability level and hope some cuties join your class. It's through doing things together that you'll get to know each other and discover if you have a lot in common. What's hard is the separation after the vacation. The boy you fall for while you're away doesn't usually live in your neighborhood at home! But with e-mail, IM—and of course, the old fashioned telephone—it's easier than ever to keep in touch. If he

doesn't say hi when he sees you on-line, well, at least you had one great week—and you don't have to worry about an embarrassing in-person rejection since he's so far away. No one will ever know! Whether or not you stay "together," the separation is painful. Unfortunately, you can be lovesick at any age. And just because you're thirteen doesn't mean your feelings aren't real. Disappointment is just something we all have to learn to deal with. It's never easy.

Here's something to help you get over your vacation crush: your birthday! A party is a perfect opportunity to get all your friends—and of course, the guy you like—in one place and have some fun outside of school. First things first: you'll need to plan some stuff to do. Just gathering everyone in the basement with some food and music could work pretty well—after all, it's the lack of parental supervision that's the real draw! But just in case, prepare some backup activities. Have a game like Twister or Taboo lying around, set up the PlayStation, or maybe even get a karaoke machine so you can all play *American Idol* if the mood strikes you. Next, think about the sound track. Ask your friends to bring all their CDs, or burn special mixes for the occasion. Include some dance songs—hey, you never know, people might actually start getting their groove on! In the beginning most of your guests will be a little intimidated—nobody wants to be the first one and risk looking dumb. But if you can convince a few other girls to get a little mini-dance-floor started with you, it might catch on. It's often the girls who have to take the initial step with these things. The guys will be relieved that you did.

what do you want to be
when you grow up?

It seems like this is the only thing adults can think to say to you lately. Which wouldn't be so bad if only you had an answer! Few people have a true "calling" in life. Some do eventually stumble across theirs, but at this point in your life, you probably find yourself changing your mind every five minutes. If you're especially good at one subject in school, it's certainly worth keeping that in mind when you think about future careers. Don't listen to the pessimists who will tell you there aren't any jobs in the field you've chosen—things might be totally different ten years down the road! Talk about your dreams with your guidance counselors and your teachers—that's what they're there for. They can tell you what subjects you'll have to do well in to achieve your goals, and give you ideas about jobs you've never thought of. You've probably got a couple years before you can take on a part-time job yourself, but if any of your relatives have a job you think is kind of cool, ask them questions about it. It might even be possible to spend a day in their office or their store to see what the work is like firsthand. You'll

also want to talk to your parents about your ideas. However, they may have different thoughts on what you should do with your future. If the career path they're pushing you toward doesn't appeal to you, tell them calmly that you'll think about it, and that you don't have to make up your mind right away . . . but don't let them talk you into it. It's up to you to choose—after all, you're the one who'll actually be doing it!

In a few years, you'll have even more opportunities to check out potential careers. For example, you can volunteer. Becoming a candy striper at a hospital will help you figure out if medicine is the right field for you. Helping build houses for Habitat for Humanity will tell you whether or not you like working with your hands. And while it's not technically volunteer work—although it usually is unpaid!—you can apply for an internship. Almost every office employs summer interns, and it's a great way to get experience in a certain industry, see if you like it, and make a few friends and connections while you're at it.

you and the world

These days, you can't ignore what's going on in the world. You might feel powerless to change any of it. But anything's possible if you set your mind to it. Begin by listening. Inform yourself. Ask questions. You have the right to know what's really happening. It's important to talk about the issues and problems facing us, because unfortunately, you'll probably have to confront them face to face at some point. You

need to be aware of things like the AIDS epidemic, for example, since one day you may be at risk. Share your point of view with your friends, but also with your parents and your doctor. Finally, convince yourself that any efforts you make are never useless, no matter how small they may seem. Not everyone can be a global activist. But there's need all around us, right here at home. Take the elderly neighbor across the street who can't get around on her own anymore—you could do her shopping, or at least say hello to her to brighten her day. People sometimes make fun of do-gooders. But these little everyday things can change the world. It's possible to make a difference at any age, and young people often put the most energy into doing just that.

you are the world

The young people of today are the adults of tomorrow. You'll be shaping the world in a few years (and in fact, you already are). Maybe politics bore you, the economy is beyond your comprehension, and the thought of war makes you sick. You don't see what you can do about any of

it. But everything that's done—good or bad—starts with the act of one individual. Think of people like Martin Luther King Jr., Abraham Lincoln, and Mother Theresa. They changed the lives of hundreds of thousands of people—maybe millions.

The difference between the present and the past is that today we're even more concerned with the lives of our fellow humans. But the world isn't getting worse, as it might seem—in fact, it's getting better, since more and more incredible, amazing people are being born each day into a time of great curiosity and communication.

It's up to you to be one of the amazing ones. The world of the future is in your hands.

Bibliography

Books
Boston Women's Health Collective. *Our Bodies, Ourselves.* New York: Simon & Schuster, 1984.

Web sites
Guide to Eyes and Vision
www.allaboutvision.com

Columbia University Health Q&A Service
www.goaskalice.columbia.edu

Health A to Z: A Family Health Site
www.healthatoz.com

KidsHealth
www.kidshealth.org

ph4

105

ph4

ph3

107

about the authors

Moka has written thirteen books for young people, published in France. She wrote *Just Us Girls* with the help of two medical specialists, a gynecologist and a physiotherapist, but her main source of inspiration was the thousands of young people she has met in France and abroad, who have shared their hopes, experiences, and anxieties with her.

Melissa Daly is a former senior staff writer at *Seventeen*, where she wrote about sex, health, and relationships. Her work has also appeared in *Marie Claire,* and she is currently associate editor at *Fitness*. She holds a degree in psychology from the College of William & Mary.